FUN UNPLUGGED

To my wonderful children, Emily and Tom, and my darling wife, Tara, who were willing assistants in helping me complete this book.

Hopefully the book can help other families and friends continue to interact with each other and have lots of fun together.

PETER COSGROVE

FUN UNPLUGGED

OUTSMART, ENTERTAIN AND AMAZE YOUR FRIENDS!

PENGUIN
IRELAND

PENGUIN IRELAND

UK | USA | Canada | Ireland | Australia
India | New Zealand | South Africa

Penguin Ireland is part of the Penguin Random House group of companies
whose addresses can be found at global.penguinrandomhouse.com.

First published by Proby Publishing 2018
Published in Penguin Ireland 2019
001

Illustrations by Amy McGrath and Alan Duffy
Cover design by Andrew Brown
Printed and bound in Great Britain by Clays Ltd, Elcograf S.p.A.

A CIP catalogue record for this book is available from the British Library

ISBN: 978–1–844–88481–0

www.greenpenguin.co.uk

CONTENTS

CHAPTER ONE

RIDDLES AND TEASERS

These are some of the trickiest riddles that are equally difficult for children and adults. There is nothing better than catching out an adult, especially since most of them think they know it all! So see how you do, and make sure you challenge lots of your friends and family with these riddles.

SPORT

1. You are participating in a race. You overtake the person in second place. What position are you in?

2. Two boxers are taking part in a boxing match (regular boxing, not kick boxing). Twelve rounds are scheduled, but the match ends after six rounds when one boxer knocks out the other boxer, yet no man throws a punch. How is this possible?

3. There are 128 players in a straight knockout tennis tournament. How many matches must be played to determine the winner?

WORDS

1. What is an eight-letter word that has only one letter in it?

2. How's your grammar? Which is correct to say: "The yolk of the egg is white" or "The yolk of the egg are white"?

3. What do you break just by saying its name?

4. What five-letter word does every English teacher pronounce wrong?

TRAVEL

1. In a movie, a plane is flying from the Bahamas to Canada. It crashes exactly on the border of the United States and Canada. Where do they bury the survivors?

2. A high-speed electric train is travelling south at 100 km/h. The wind is blowing westward at 10 km/h. In which direction does the smoke blow?

3. Pretend you are a bus driver. At your first stop a kid, a lawyer and a mother with her baby get on. At the next stop a judge, a kid and his dad going to a baseball game get on. At the third stop a skater, a golfer and footballer get on. Three people get off at the fourth stop. What is the name of the bus driver?

4. A man got married and took a train the next day. On the train every single passenger fell asleep, but he did not. Why?

5. John and Jim were in a plane 100 km off the coast of Ireland. John bet Jim that if he threw a 5 kg steel ball out of the plane six seconds after John threw a 5 kg sack of feathers out of the plane, the ball would hit the ground first. Which of the two would actually hit the ground first?

6. A ship is at anchor. Over the side of the ship hangs a ladder with nine half-metre rungs. The tide rises half a metre per hour. After five hours, how many rungs will be above the water, assuming all nine rungs were above the water before the tide began to rise?

NUMBERS

1. Professor Clink has two coins that total 25 cents. If one of the coins is not a 5-cent coin, how is this possible?

2. If seven people meet and each shakes hands only once with each other, how many handshakes will there be?

3. A woman has seven children and half of them are boys. How is this possible?

4. Two fathers and two sons go fishing together in the same boat. They all catch a fish but the total catch for the day is three fish. How is this possible?

5. How many times can you subtract five from twenty-five?

6. How many cubic metres of dirt are there in a hole, 6 metres long, 2 metres wide and 1 metre deep?

7. If a doctor gives you three pills and tells you to take one every half hour, how long will the pills last?

8. A tree doubled in height every year until it reached its maximum height in ten years. How many years did it take to reach half of its maximum height?

9. A boy eats sherbet straws by sucking the sherbet out of the straw. There is always some sherbet left at the end that he cannot get out. After having seven sherbet straws he can open them up and make one extra sherbet straw from the leftovers. He has kept a box of 49 sherbet straws that he has sucked. How many sherbet straws can he make from the leftovers?

FOOD

1. A woman decided to make herself a cup of coffee. Her clip-on earring fell into the cup. Even though the cup had coffee in it, the earring did not get wet. How?

2. What two things can you not have for breakfast?

3. A magician is standing on a concrete floor, holding a raw egg in his outstretched hand. Without any aids he is able to drop the egg 2 metres without breaking the shell. How?

4. A basket contains five apples. Can you divide the apples among five boys so that each boy gets an apple and one apple stays in the basket?

5. John walked out of a restaurant and it started to rain. He had no hat, coat or umbrella and his clothes got soaked. Yet not one hair on his head got wet. How is this possible?

6. If you take two apples from three apples, how many will you have?

ANIMALS

1. A completely black horse jumped over a tower and landed on a small man who then disappeared. In what situation is this possible?

2. Which of these three would see most clearly in total darkness: a leopard, a bat or an owl?

3. Polar bears, seals and penguins all live in polar regions. Polar bears hunt seals but never penguins. Why is this?

4. There are twenty sick sheep in a field and six of them have to be taken to the vet. How many are left? (Tip: this one only works if you read it aloud to someone.)

5. A frog sits on a lily in the middle of a lake. He is 20 metres from the edge of the lake and his first jump takes him 10 metres to the next lily. After this, each jump takes him half the distance, so his next jump is 5 metres. How many more jumps for him to get to the edge?

6. How far can a dog run into the woods?

WATER

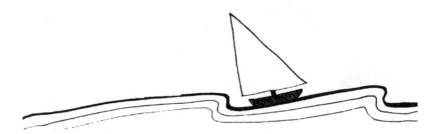

1. If you drop a white hat into the Red Sea, what will it become?

2. Answer this one quickly. What would you prefer to be: nearly saved or nearly drowned?

3. Thirty people jumped into an empty swimming pool and dived under. None were pregnant or conjoined twins, yet thirty foreheads came up. How is this possible? (Tip: Read this aloud quickly.)

4. Imagine you are stuck on a block of ice 1,000 km from anyone, with no boat, no phone and no one knows you are there. How do you get back home?

THE HUMAN BODY

1. How would you describe a man who does not have all his fingers on his left hand?

2. Can you name eleven body parts that are spelt with only three letters? These are all words in the dictionary and you will know them all. No slang words allowed!

3. What is harder to catch the faster you run?

19

TIME

1. In a year there are 12 months. Seven months have 31 days. How many months have 28 days?

2. Nelly Nirtle's birthday is on 27 December but her birthday is always in the summer, how is this possible?

3. A teacher said there are 12 seconds in a year and she was correct. How could this be?

4. Two girls were born to the same mother, on the same day, in the same month and year, and yet they are not twins. How can this be?

5. What question can someone ask all day long and always get completely different answers and yet all the answers are correct?

6. Mr Bell has a clock that chimes once on the half hour and once for one o'clock, twice for two o'clock, three times for three o'clock, etc. One day he walks in and hears the clock chime once. Half an hour later it chimes once. Half an hour later it chimes once, and half an hour later it chimes once. If the clock is not broken how is it possible, and what time did he enter his house?

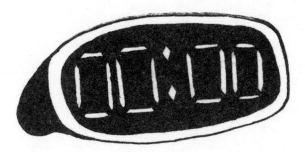

MISCELLANEOUS

1. If the lights went off in a house and you had a large yellow candle, a medium size green candle and a small white candle, what would you light first?

2. A man and his son were rock-climbing. The man slipped and fell to his death and the son was badly injured and rushed to hospital. At the hospital, the old surgeon looked at the young man and declared, "I can't operate on this boy. He is my son." How can this be?

3. Before Mount Everest was discovered, what was the highest mountain on earth?

4. A cowboy rode into town on Friday. He stayed two nights and left on Friday. How is this possible without a time machine?

5. A man buys rice at €1 per kilogram from a grower in India and sells the rice at 50 cent per kilogram in India. As a result of this he becomes a millionaire. How is this possible?

6. If a red house is made of red bricks and a blue house is made of blue bricks and a yellow house is made of yellow bricks, what is a greenhouse made of?

7. A racquet and a ball cost €1.10 in total. The racquet costs €1.00 more than the ball. How much does the ball cost?

8. One knight a baker, a butcher and a bus driver went into an empty castle (none of them were pregnant). One hour later four people came out of the castle. Who were they? (Tip: This one works better if you read this out loud to someone.)

CHAPTER TWO

TRICKS OF THE MIND

The puzzles in this section take more thought and time, but people will feel great if they get the answer right. The answers may not be obvious, so give your friends time and a pen and paper to work them out. They still won't, though! Some of these tricks of the mind will make people think you've attended a wizardry course!

PUZZLE 1
COUNT THE F'S

Show these three lines to a friend and ask them to read the sentence and to count the number of F's in the sentence. Tell them to take 30 seconds so they can read it nice and slowly.

Finished files are the result of months of scientific study combined with the experience of years.

PUZZLE 2
READ THIS SENTENCE

Show a friend this sentence and ask them if they can detect anything odd about it.

Please can you read the

following sentence and tell me

me if you see

anything

funny?

PUZZLE 3
CONNECT THE DOTS

Draw out nine dots like in the picture below and ask someone to connect all nine dots, following these rules: they can only draw straight lines and the pen must never be taken off the page. Annoy them by telling them that you can do it with four lines. If they get it right, annoy them further by saying you can do it in three lines!

PUZZLE 4

UNUSUAL SENTENCE

Ask someone what is so unusual about the sentence below, apart from the fact that it does not make a lot of sense.

JACKDAWS

LOVE MY

BIG SPHINX

OF QUARTZ

PUZZLE 5
UNUSUAL PARAGRAPH

Give the following paragraph to someone to read and answer the question that is asked:

This is an unusual paragraph. I'm curious how quickly you can find out what is so unusual about it. It looks so plain you would think nothing was wrong with it. In fact, nothing is wrong with it! It is unusual though. Study it, and think about it, but you still may not find anything odd. But if you work at it a bit, you might find out! You may not at first find anything particularly odd or unusual or in any way dissimilar to any ordinary paragraph. Good luck!

PUZZLE 6
A THOUSAND ADDITIONS

Ask a friend to add up some simple numbers in their head. When they are ready call the additions out as follows:

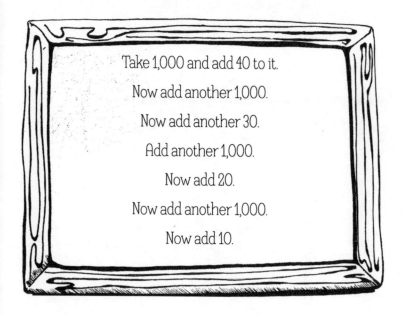

Take 1,000 and add 40 to it.

Now add another 1,000.

Now add another 30.

Add another 1,000.

Now add 20.

Now add another 1,000.

Now add 10.

What is the total?

PUZZLE 7
NINE INTO SIX

Take a pen and paper and draw the Roman numeral IX. Show it to a friend and ask if they are familiar with Roman numerals. If they are, they will say that IX represents nine. Now ask them to change this into a six with one stroke of the pen.

PUZZLE 8

ONE LINE AND
A NEW NUMBER

Write down the problem below on a piece of paper. Ask a friend to add one straight line to change this puzzle so that it is correct, and the one thing they cannot do is put a line through the equals sign (=) to make it a does-not-equal sign(≠).

$$5 + 5 + 5 = 550$$

PUZZLE 9

MISSING NUMBER

Write down this number sequence on a piece of paper and show it to a friend. Ask them what number goes in the blank.

16, 06, 68, 88, ___, 98?

PUZZLE 10
HARDWARE PROBLEM

A man went to the hardware store to buy items for his house.

He asked the assistant, "How much would one cost?"

He was told €5.00.

He then asked, "How much would 22 cost?"

He was told €10.00.

Finally he asked how much for 122, and he was told that this would cost €15.00.

What was he buying?

PUZZLE 11
THE 9 BALLS PROBLEM

You must identify one ball out of nine. There are nine identical-looking balls in front of you and all you have is a balance scales. Each ball is equally big and equally heavy, except for one, which is a little heavier. You will not be able to do this by holding the balls in your hand. How can you identify the heavier ball if you can use the balance scales only twice?

PUZZLE 12
LIGHT–BULB PROBLEM

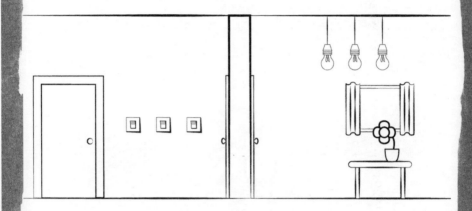

You are standing in a hallway next to three light switches, which are all in the off position. There is another room down the hallway, which contains three light bulbs. Each light bulb is operated by one of the switches next to you. From where you are standing in the hallway, you cannot see the bulbs because they are in the other room.

How would you figure out which switch operates which light bulb? You can flick the switches on and off as many times as you want. However, you can go into the room with the light bulbs only once.

PUZZLE 13
4 LITRES

You have a tap and two jugs. One of the jugs holds 3 litres, and the other holds 5 litres. You have to measure exactly 4 litres of water using only these two jugs.

PUZZLE 14
READ THEIR MIND

Tell your friend that you are going to attempt to read their mind but to do this you will have to ask them some questions, which they must answer very quickly.

Start with some simple additions.

$$1 + 5 \ (6)$$
$$2 + 2 \ (4)$$
$$3 + 3 \ (6)$$
$$4 + 4 \ (8)$$
$$5 + 1 \ (6)$$

Now ask them to say the number 6 to themselves as fast as they can for 10 seconds.

Now tell them to quickly think of a vegetable and write it down.

Ask them if they are thinking of carrots (most people are!)

PUZZLE 15
THINK OF AN OBJECT

This is another mind-reading one! Ask a friend to play along as you ask them some simple maths puzzles.

How much is:

15 + 6 (21)

3 + 56 (59)

89 + 2 (91)

12 + 53 (65)

75 + 26 (101)

25 + 52 (77)

63 + 32 (95)

Then say, "Hang in there. It's nearly over!"

121 + 7 (128)

Now ask them to quickly think of a tool and the colour of that tool and write it down. Ask them if they are thinking about a red hammer.

PUZZLE 16
THINK OF A NUMBER

Write down the number 7 on a piece of paper and turn it over. Now ask your friend these sums:

2+2 (4)
3+3 (6)
4+4 (8)
8+8 (16)
16+16 (32)

Now tell them to quickly pick a number between 12 and 5 and shout it out. Show them the piece of paper that you have already written the number 7 on.

PUZZLE 17
COLOUR COUNTRY ANIMAL

Ask your friend to follow these instructions:

Think of a number between 2 and 9.

Multiply the number by 9.

Add the two numbers together (e.g. 63 (6 + 3) would become 9).

Take away 5 from the total.

They will now have a single number in their head.

Ask them to make the number into a letter. So 1 = A, 2 = B, 3 = C, etc.

Ask them to choose a country beginning with that letter.

Once they have done this, ask them to think of the second letter in the country and think of an animal that begins with that letter.

Finally ask them to think of a colour for that animal.

Now tell them that they are thinking of a grey elephant from Denmark, and they will look at you with shock and awe!

PUZZLE 18

COAST

Ask a friend if they can follow instructions and answer a simple question.

Tell them to say the word "coast" 10 times, fast. Once they are finished, ask them this question: "What do you put in a toaster?"

PUZZLE 19
SILK

Ask a friend if they can follow instructions and answer a simple question.

Tell them to say the word "silk" 10 times, fast. Once they are finished, ask them this question: "What do cows drink?"

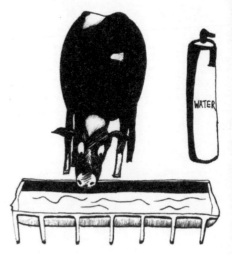

PUZZLE 20
SMART OR DUMB

Ask a friend, "Are you smart or dumb?"

They will naturally say, "Smart!"

You say, "Okay, I will test you."

Ask them:

What is 2 + 2 (4)

What is 3 + 3 (6)

What is 4 + 4 (8)

What is 5 + 5 (10)

What is 10 + 10 (20)

Then ask them: "What was the first question I asked you?"

CHAPTER 3

OUTSMART YOUR FAMILY AND FRIENDS

Do you know a smarty-pants who has all the answers? Well, this time they won't be smiling! Here are some tricks that you can play on anyone. Some of these take a little practice but it will be worth it to see the look on the other person's face!

17 PENNIES

THE CHALLENGE

Put down 17 coins in the middle of the table. Tell your friend that the rules are as follows: You each take turns to remove coins from the pile in the middle and you have to remove one, two or three coins when it is your turn. Take turns removing either one, two or three coins. The loser is the person who has to take out the last coin. Have a practice go first and let them win. After that, start taking bets!

THE TRICK

Always ensure that your opponent goes first. The trick is to make sure that, between the two of you, exactly four coins are removed in each round. So if your opponent takes out three coins, you take out one. If they take out two, you take out two. If they take out one, you take out three. They will always be left with one, so you will always win!

COUNT TO 10 BACKWARDS

THE CHALLENGE

Bet someone that they cannot count from 10 to 1 backwards. Stress to them that they cannot make any mistakes (as if the pressure will make them stumble!). They will think it is easy and carefully count back from 10 to 1. When they finish, tell them they have failed and that they should have listened to the question!

THE TRICK

They did not listen to the question. You asked them to count from 10 to 1 backwards, so they should have started from 1 and gone up to 10, not from 10 to 1. When you stress that they must not stumble over their words, they pay little attention to the wording of the question!

TALLEST MOUNTAIN

THE CHALLENGE

Tell someone you know that you can ask them a question and they will get it wrong. Tell them you will even tell them the question in advance. They will be suspicious, but if they agree, ask them: "What is the tallest mountain in the world?"

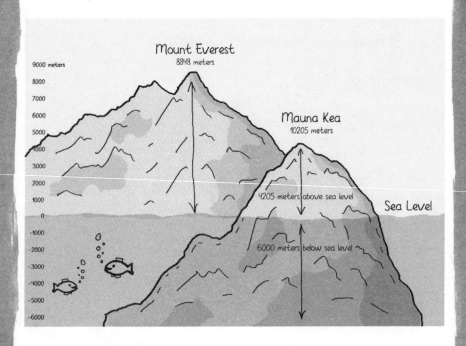

THE TRICK

Most people will look at you strangely and then say Mount Everest. Tell them that unfortunately Mount Everest is the highest mountain in the world, but the tallest is Mount Mauna Kea (two-thirds of it is under water, but from bottom to top it is a lot taller than Mount Everest).

TIP

To annoy them even more, ask them the following: "You are correct that Mount Everest is the highest mountain in the world but do you know what the highest mountain in the world was before Mount Everest was discovered?" When they give you an answer or when they are stumped, tell them the answer is Mount Everest - it was still the highest even though it had not been discovered!

SPEAKING WITHOUT USING THE LETTER "A"

THE CHALLENGE

Talk to your friends and see how long they can speak for, in normal sentences, without using the letter "A". Everyone will find this very difficult, even when they talk slowly. After a while, tell them you think you could do it and bet your friend that you can speak for a full minute at a normal speed and make total sense, without using the letter "A". The rules are that you cannot just repeat a word and you must make sense and speak at a normal pace. They will think this is impossible and bet you cannot do it.

THE TRICK

This is a clever one. There is no letter "A" in the first 999 numbers, as long as you say "one hundred one" and not "one hundred and one", etc. So start by saying, "I will now count out loud for you. One, two, three, four . . ." Just keep going! You can go all day, much longer than one minute, and much to the annoyance of your friends.

COIN AND CUP - READ THEIR MIND

THE CHALLENGE

Put a 10-cent coin under a cup and tell your friend that you can get the coin into your pocket without touching or moving the cup. Ensure you have a second 10-cent coin in your pocket already.

THE TRICK

Once your friend agrees, move your hand around the cup a few times (without touching the cup) and then say "There!" and take a coin out of your pocket. They won't believe you and will probably pick up the cup. You then grab the coin under the cup without having to touch the cup!

WHICH IS LONGER?

THE CHALLENGE

This is an amazing optical illusion. Take a pint glass and ask someone which is longer, the circumference of the top of the glass (this is the distance around the rim of the glass) or the height of the glass. Before they can answer, put a cup under the pint glass and ask if the circumference of the top of the glass is longer than the height of the cup and the glass combined. Most people will say the height is definitely longer than the circumference.

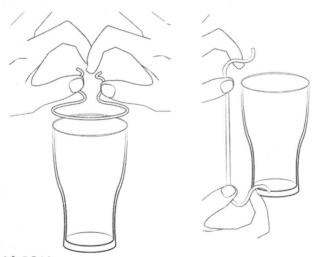

THE TRICK

There is no trick! It is just an amazing optical illusion. The circumference of nearly any glass is longer then its length, even very tall, thin glasses. Just take a piece of thread and measure.

FOUR COINS

THE CHALLENGE

Put four coins in a diamond shape. The task is to change them from a diamond to a straight line. The rules are that you can move one coin at a time and every time you let go of a coin it must be touching two other coins. Also, you are not allowed to push a coin into another coin.

So you move from: To:

THE TRICK

This is tricky, although it sounds easy. It goes in four steps. The white coin is the coin that you have just moved each time.

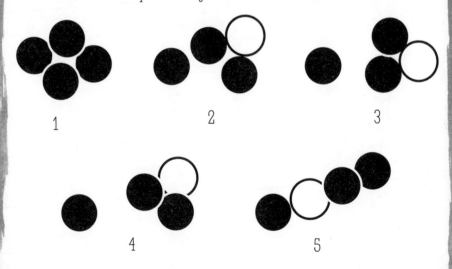

FOLLOW YOUR LEAD

THE CHALLENGE

Give your friend a glass of water and take one for yourself. Tell your friend that they will not be able to follow your lead. All they have to do is copy everything you do.

» Take a sip of your drink and raise your glass in the air and say, "To Neptune!"

» Then take a second sip of your drink and raise it again and say, "To Poseidon!"

» Finally, drink the rest of your water, raise your glass in the air and say nothing.

» Now lower your glass and proceed to spit out some of the water that you intentionally did not swallow.

Cheers!

THE TRICK

Your friend will not know that you have kept water in your mouth, and therefore will not be able to copy you.

A second trick is to do this on someone who has seen the trick but does not know that you know they have seen it. They therefore think they are going to fool you! Follow the trick as before with one difference. This time when you spit out, you only spit out some of the drink in your mouth. So when your friend does the same and thinks he has won, raise your glass again and spit out for the second time. Your friend will be furious!

BOOK TRICK

THE CHALLENGE

Take two books and give one to your friend. Start to flick through your book and ask them to say stop. When they do, tell them the page number you have stopped at. Ask them to open up the book in their hand to the same page number. Now ask them to look at the biggest word on the top line and think of that word. Think very hard and the word will magically come to you!

THE TRICK

» Pick up a book and start to flick through it casually. When you get to the middle of the book, find a big word in the top line of the page and remember both the word and the page number (this may take a little practice).

» Now put the two books down and ask your friend to pick one. If it is the one you have just looked at, tell them to take it and to pass the other one to you. If they pick up the book you have not looked at, take it and give them the other book.

» Now tell them that you will flick through the pages until they say stop. Most people say stop after two to four seconds, so no matter what page you land on, say the page number you have memorised. No one ever checks your book page.

» Now tell them to go to that page in their book. When they look for the biggest word, you will know it as long as your memory does not fail you!

TIP

If your friend takes too long to stay stop, flick quickly to the end of the book and tell them they need to say stop quicker.

BOOK TRICK WITH NUMBERS

THE CHALLENGE

This can be done anywhere there are books and only takes a little bit of work. Ask someone to pick a three-digit number where the first and last digit differ by two or more, say 478 (so they cannot pick 484 as the first and last digits are not two numbers apart). Now tell them you are going to test their maths skills.

» Pick a number (first and last digits need to be 2 apart at least, so not 323 or 433, for example).

» Have them reverse their number.

» Tell them to take the smaller from the larger number.

» Now ask them to reverse this number and add the two together.

» Tell them they should have a 4-digit number. The first three numbers are to represent a page in a book and the fourth number is the number of words they count before they land on the chosen word. They choose a book, go to the page and count across to the word. Ask them to concentrate on the word and then magically tell them what the word is!

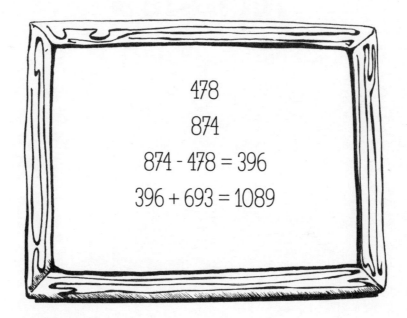

478

874

874 - 478 = 396

396 + 693 = 1089

THE TRICK

The great part of this is the way you get them to pick the number. It will always be 1,089. Knowing this, you need to do a little bit of preparation. Have two books in front of you. You will have already gone to page 108 in both books and memorised the ninth word on the first line. Simple!

Remember, this will not work if the person is bad at maths!

COFFEE HOLDER ILLUSION

THE CHALLENGE

This works in any coffee shop. Take two coffee holders and tell your friend that you know one is bigger than the other, but they will not be able to guess which. Open up the two coffee holders (called "zarfs", by the way) and write an A on one and a B on the other. Ask your friend to pick which is bigger. After they pick, put the coffee holders down one above the other to show them they are wrong.

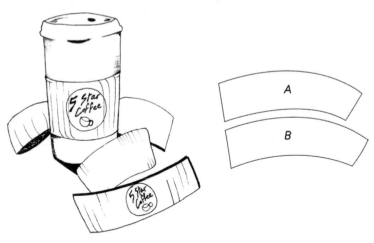

THE TRICK

They are obviously the same size, but it does not look like that when you put one above the other. So whichever one they pick as the larger one, put that on the top and the other one will always look bigger. Try it!

WHAT'S THE TIME?

THE CHALLENGE

Tell an adult who has a traditional (not digital) watch that you are going to ask them three questions about their watch. Tell them the questions will be very simple but you still think they will get one wrong.

First ask: "Does your watch have a second hand?" Most people will get this right.

Second ask: "Does your watch have the number three?" Some watches have Roman numerals so they may need to think about it but will more than likely get it right.

Finally ask: "Without looking at your watch again, what is the exact time?"

THE TRICK

Amazingly, many people will have looked at their watch but not seen what the time is, and you will win. You will not win every time but it should work most times.

ANAGRAM FINDER

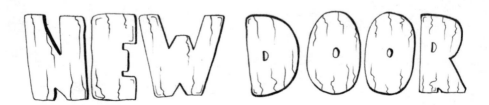

THE CHALLENGE

Write out the words NEW DOOR in large, black upper-case letters and ask an adult to arrange the letters to create one word. They must use all the letters.

THE TRICK

The trick is annoying as the clue is in the question. You cannot create one word from these letters. However, you can arrange them into "ONE WORD", which is exactly what you asked them to do!

CATCH A €20 NOTE

THE CHALLENGE

Hold out a €20 note between your thumb and middle finger and tell someone to put their hand in a "holding a glass" shape around the note. Tell them you will drop the note through their hand three times and all they need to do is catch it as it drops. Do it yourself to show that it can be done quite easily. The only rule is that if they close their hands before you drop it, they lose (you don't want them to anticipate when you let go of the note). Also, they cannot move their arm downwards. The only thing they can move is their hand.

THE TRICK

Very few people have the reflexes to do this. But you can do it yourself very easily when you demonstrate, as you know when you are dropping the €20 note, so you know when to close your hand. It is very different when someone else is dropping the note. So demonstrate first and then tell your friend they can keep the money if they catch the note, but they have to give you money if they don't.

GUESS THE NUMBER

THE CHALLENGE

Ask someone to think of a number between 1 and 100 and tell them they cannot change their number. Tell them you will guess the number correctly on the first try. Mention to them that you have the number written down in your pocket already.

THE TRICK

Write down the number 1 on a piece of paper and put it in your pocket. Once your friend has picked a number, ask them to think of it in their mind. Ask them, "Are you thinking of one?" They will say yes because it sounds like you are just asking them if they are thinking of a number! Then you show them the number 1, and don't listen to any protests!

THE THREE CUP TRICK

THE CHALLENGE

Label three cups A, B and C and place them beside each other. Place cup A mouth downwards, cup B mouth upwards and cup C mouth downwards. Tell your friend that within three moves – always moving two cups at a time – you can finish with all three cups facing upwards. Then show them how, and do it slowly. Turn B and C, then Turn A and C, and then turn B and C. You will finish with all three

cups mouth upwards. Now ask them to try. They will keep finishing with all the cups facing downwards, not upwards.

THE TRICK

When you set up the cups for your friend, place the cups in the opposite starting position, so two are mouth upwards and the middle one is mouth downwards. No one notices!

5 SQUARES TO 6

THE CHALLENGE

Put out 12 matches into 4 squares as per the diagram below and ask people to move 2 matches and change the diagram from 5 squares to 6 squares.

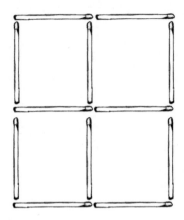

THE TRICK

Take 2 of the matches from the middle and place them as per the diagram. Simple!

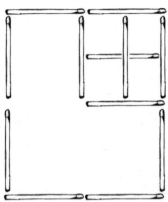

SALTY ICE

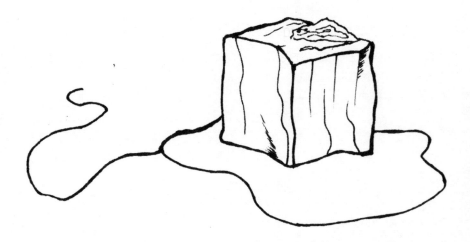

THE CHALLENGE

You will need two glasses, two lengths of thread, two ice cubes and some salt. Tell someone that you can remove an ice cube from a glass using just the thread. You cannot touch the glass or the ice cube with your hands. This is almost impossible, so they will presume neither of you can do it. Let them try first with their glass, length of thread and ice cube in the glass.

THE TRICK

Take the thread and rest it on the ice cube. Put some salt on top of the thread and the ice cube. The salt will quickly freeze and you will be able to pull the cube out with the thread. Hey presto!

STRAW ON A BOTTLE

THE CHALLENGE

Place a straw on a bottle and ask a friend to make the straw move without blowing it or touching it. When they fail, just show them how.

THE TRICK

When your friend looks away take the straw off the bottle and rub it on your clothes. Then place it on the bottle again. As you put your finger close to the straw you will see it move. It's called static electricity.

TOILET ROLL

THE CHALLENGE

Give a friend a cardboard toilet-roll tube or a cork from a wine bottle (as long as it is still fairly much intact). Ask them to drop it on the table so that it lands standing up. They will keep trying to drop it and it will land on its side.

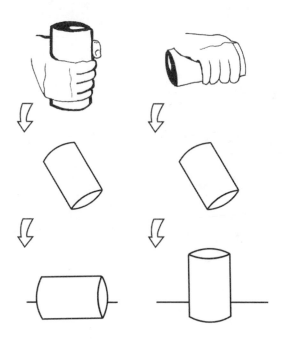

THE TRICK

When you are dropping the toilet-roll tube, hold it on its side horizontally, and not vertically. There is a very good chance that it will land standing up, although it may take a few tries.

SIX GLASSES

THE CHALLENGE

Put six glasses on a table. Have the first three full of liquid and the next three empty. Ask someone to change the order to full, empty, full, empty, full, empty, just by touching one glass. They will not be able to.

THE TRICK

Take the second full glass and pour the liquid into the fifth glass, which does the trick!

CRAYONS IN A RESTAURANT

THE CHALLENGE

Often, there are crayons for younger kids in a restaurant. Tell a friend that the colours mean the crayons are different weights and you can tell which colour a crayon is without looking. Hold one hand behind your back and tell them to take out a crayon and put it in your hand. Tell them to hide the rest of the crayons. After holding the crayon for a few seconds behind your back, have them take it back and amaze them by telling them the colour.

THE TRICK

Discretely dig a nail into the crayon while you are holding it behind your back. Quickly check your nail to see what colour the crayon is as you bring your hand up to wipe your nose.

NEWSPAPER TRICK

THE CHALLENGE

Tell someone you can stand on one end of a newspaper and if they stand on the other side they will be unable to touch you. They will think that this is impossible and may think the trick is the size of the newspaper. Show them that it is a normal-size newspaper.

THE TRICK

Place the newspaper down in a doorway, have your friend stand on it and then close the door. When you stand on your side, they will be unable to touch you!

MATCH/ PITCHFORK

THE CHALLENGE

Take out four matches and make them into a shape of a pitch fork. Put a coin in the fork and ask if anyone can get the coin out without touching it, keeping the pitchfork in the same shape and only touching two matches.

THE TRICK

Slide B across to the right and then take A to the new position. You have now inverted the fork and the coin is outside.

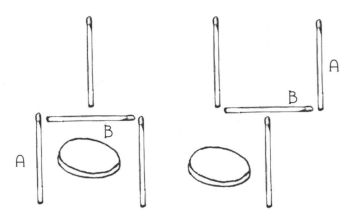

MOVING STRAW TRICK

THE CHALLENGE

This is one of my all-time favourite tricks, as it always has everyone scratching their heads. For this you just need half a straw. Put the straw on the table and tell your friends you can move it without touching it. You want them to focus on the straw, so here is where you need to do a little acting. Circle the straw with your fingers, rub under the table and eventually put your thumb close to the straw and move your thumb away from your body. The straw will magically follow your thumb, to the shock of your friends.

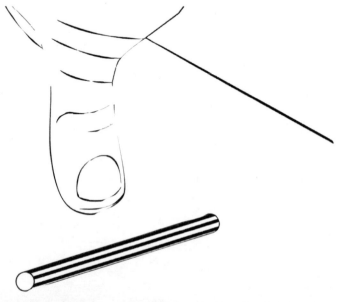

THE TRICK

Like all tricks, this one is obvious once you know how it works. Nevertheless, this trick baffles people, especially if you only do it once or twice and don't give them a chance to watch it multiple times. The key is all the work you do rubbing underneath the table and around the straw as you talk about your magical powers. As you pull your thumb away everyone is watching in amazement as the straw moves. No one notices that you are blowing gently and that is what is moving the straw! No one looks at your mouth because they are paying attention to the straw. But do blow gently or they will be able to hear you.

TIP

Make sure the straw is small and light, or you can use anything that is light and rolls easily.

FLOATING BREAD ROLL

THE CHALLENGE

When you sit down for dinner and are waiting for your main course, demonstrate how you can make a bread roll float above your napkin.

THE TRICK

Stick a fork into the bottom of a bread roll and then hold up a napkin with your two hands. Hold the handle of the fork between the finger and thumb of one of your hands. It will look to the dinner guests as if you are holding the napkin at each corner, using both your hands, so you couldn't possibly be holding a fork as well.

Then gradually raise the bread roll above the napkin by moving the fork handle upwards using your hidden thumb, to show a floating bread roll. Make sure to keep the fork below the napkin. You can float it up and then down again a few times. While your family looks on in amazement, take the bread roll off the fork and take a bite out of it to finish.

READ THEIR MINDS

THE CHALLENGE

Tell the group that you and your friend can read each other's minds and to prove it you will leave the room and have another person point at anything in the room. When you are asked back in, your friend will keep pointing at items in the room and you will say "yes" once he points at the correct item, to the gasps of your friends.

THE TRICK

How does it work? Agree with your friend that before they point at the correct item they will first always point at something black. If the group works this out, you can use a second method. Agree in advance that the item he picks will be the same number as the number of words he says when you come back in. So, when you come in, if he says "Good luck!" it will be the second item he points at. If he says "They think you will fail", it will be the fifth item. You now have two different ways, and the group will never work it out.

9 COINS

THE CHALLENGE

Tell your friend you will ask them some simple number questions and that you will read their mind and guess the number.

» Ask your friend to think of any two-digit number.

» Then ask them to add the two numbers together and take the answer from the first number. For example, if they pick the number 53, then they add 5 + 3 = 8 and the answer from 53, so 53 - 8 = 45.

» Ask them to add those two numbers together so they have a single-digit number. In our example, it would be 4 + 5 = 9.

$$95$$
$$9 + 5 = 14$$
$$95 - 14 = 81$$
$$8 + 1 = 9$$

$$42$$
$$4 + 2 = 6$$
$$42 - 6 = 36$$
$$3 + 6 = 9$$

» Now tell them that the number you have is the same as the number of coins you have in your hand. You open your hand to display nine coins!

THE TRICK

This is a maths trick that always works. The answer will always be 9, whatever number they start with. So as long as you have 9 coins in your hand, you will always win.

TIP

If you can manage to get someone to cut a one-cent coin in half you can win big on this trick! When you get to the end of the trick and they have the number 9 in their head, ask them to divide their answer by two. When you say "I bet you I have the same number of coins in my pocket," they will not believe you because their number contains a half. They will bet you anything, maybe even their pocket money! Have a look at their face when they say four and a half and you open up your hand to show them four one-cent coins and a half a one-cent coin!

MATCHBOX TRICK

THE CHALLENGE

You will need four matchboxes, some matches and a rubber band. Put three matchboxes (two empty and one with matches in it) in front of an adult and ask them which one has matches in it. When they tell you it's impossible to tell, you just shake the three matchboxes until you hear the rattle of matches in one of them. They will feel a little foolish, but then you say you will start again. This time you shake the matchboxes at the start and then move them around. This will make them think that they can easily pick the right one. But when you ask them to choose, they will pick the wrong one.

THE TRICK

You will have a fourth matchbox with some matches in it attached to your wrist using a rubber band, with your sleeve rolled down over it. So when you pick up one of the empty boxes and shake it (with the arm that has the hidden matchbox), they will hear matches and think that this is the matchbox with the matches. You then move them around slowly enough that they can follow. Guess what! They will pick the wrong one!

LEVITATING A PERSON

THE CHALLENGE

Have a friend lie down and put a sheet over him or her. Tell everyone that you will now levitate them, and watch the amazed look of your friends when it starts to happen as you raise your hands, making chanting noises.

THE TRICK

Have a friend lie down on their back. When you are holding the sheet up and before you lay it over your friend, ensure that your friend is hidden from view for a second or two. In that time they will move from lying on their back to lying on their belly. When you start chanting, your friend will slowly move up onto their knees, extend one leg horizontally and one arm in the opposite direction. This makes it look like their whole body is levitating.

TIP

Do a couple of practice runs first. Make sure everyone is watching from the same direction so they cannot peek around the side of the sheet.

LEVITATING A CUP

THE CHALLENGE

Hold a takeaway coffee cup with two hands and then magically remove both your hands and the cup will remain in the air and move slightly towards the other person. As you are doing this, also distract your friend by pretending the whole thing is freaking you out.

THE TRICK

Punch a little hole in the cup at the back out of their view and have your thumb in it. Have a paper cup in two hands and push the cup towards them as you take your hands off the cup so it looks like the cup is levitating. Add a line like "I knew coffee gave you energy, but I did not think it was this type of energy!"

COIN TRICK

THE CHALLENGE

Place six coins on a table in two lines of three. Tell a friend that you can guess which coin he has chosen and turn your back or leave the room. When you come back stare at the six coins and magically pick up the right one. They will ask you to leave again and will be annoyed when you come back and pick the right one again!

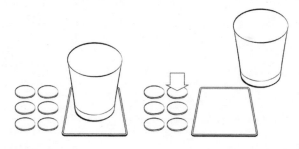

THE TRICK

You need an accomplice who no one else is aware of and you will have planned this trick well in advance, so when you are there no one even knows you are working together. Your friend can pretend to be challenging you as if they are trying to work out the trick, but they will be secretly helping you. Your friend needs a drink to be on a coaster and when you leave the room and a coin is picked he or she takes a drink and then puts the drink down in one of six positions around the coaster, which represent the six positions of the coins. No one notices someone who is taking a drink.

TORN NAPKIN

THE CHALLENGE

Take a napkin, hand it to someone and ask them to tear it into four or six pieces. When they have done this, ask them to ball up all of the tissue pieces into one ball, as small as possible. Now show them one of your fists, which is lightly clenched, and ask them to push the ripped-up tissue into your fist until it disappears. Turn your wrist over and start to take the tissue out from the other end. Then hand it back to them and ask them to open it up gently. They will be amazed that the tissue is back in one piece.

THE TRICK

Most tissues have two layers to them, and you can carefully separate them. Take one half and hide it at the bottom of your closed fist. Hand the other piece to your friend to rip up. When you pull the tissue out of the bottom of your fist, it is actually the one you had hidden there, and the ripped one remains in your fist. When you ask your friend to open up the tissue, tell them to be very careful. While they are focusing on doing this, you can dispose of the ripped-up tissue. They won't even notice!

BROKEN THUMB

THE CHALLENGE

Tell everyone that you are going to break your own thumb by pulling it backwards and watch them squeal as they hear a noise that sounds like you are breaking your thumb.

THE TRICK

All you will need for this is a small plastic cup. You will find lots of them by any office water coolers. Put the plastic cup under your elbow, resting it against your body. As you pull your thumb up with your other hand, squeeze your elbow against your body to make the breaking noise, CRACK! which will scare your friends! Plastic cups will really only work once.

CALENDAR MEMORY

THE CHALLENGE

Show everyone that you can learn the whole calendar off by heart. Tell someone to pick a month and a date, and then within five seconds tell them the day of the week that this falls on.

THE TRICK

This takes memory and someone who is good with numbers. It is very rewarding if you can master it in front of friends and family. Memorise the date of the first Monday of every month of the year. So in 2019, 7 January is the first Monday, 4 February is the first Monday and then 4 March, 1 April, 6 May, 3 June, 1 July, 5 August, 2 September, 7 October, 4 November and 2 December. This gives you the sequence: 7, 4, 4, 1, 6, 3, 1, 5, 2, 7, 4, 2.

Once you memorise this sequence, if someone then asks what day 24 September will fall on, you know that the first Monday of September is a 2. So, going up in sevens, you know that 9 September, 16 September and 23 September are all Mondays. Add one and you know that 24 September is a Tuesday.

With a little practice you can become very quick at his. Always ask your friend to say the month first and then the day, as once they say the month you can start working it out in your head.

I LOST MY TEETH!

THE CHALLENGE

In view of others, pretend to trip and fall into a wall. Wail in pain and then spit out what looks like your teeth. Be ready for your parents to go bananas!

THE TRICK

Chew some mints and make sure they are in small pieces in your mouth. When you hit the wall, spit out the mints and they will look like your teeth. This is a great trick for April Fool's Day.

CHAPTER FOUR

HILARIOUS
JOKES

No book that challenges the mind should ignore the funny bone! This chapter contains the corniest jokes that are guaranteed to make people laugh! Pick your favourites and see if your friends agree.

Why wouldn't the crab share his food?

Because he was a little shellfish.

Two sausages in a frying pan. One says to the other, "Wow! It's hot in here."

The other says, "Oh my God! A talking sausage!"

A man walks into a bar.

Ouch!

What do you call a dinosaur with a sore bum?

Megasoras.

What's orange and sounds like a carrot?

A parrot.

What do you call shoes made of bananas?

Slippers.

Why did the man put the clock in the safe?

To save time.

How do you kill a circus?

Go for the juggler.

Why does a golfer wear two pair of pants?

In case he gets a hole in one.

How do hedgehogs play leapfrog?

Very carefully.

Why can't you tell a joke while ice-skating?

The ice might crack up.

Why do gorillas have big nostrils?

To fit their big fingers up their nose!

What did the submarine say to the ship?

I can see your bottom.

What does a policeman say to his tummy?

You're under a vest.

Teacher: "Johnny you missed school yesterday, didn't you?"

Johnny: "No, not really!"

What would you do if an elephant sat in front of you at the movies?

You would miss most of the film.

Why don't they play poker in the jungle?

Too many cheetahs.

Why don't dogs make good dancers?

Because they have two left feet.

Teacher: "Name six wild animals."

Pupil: "Four tigers and two elephants."

What time is it when an elephant sits on your fence?

Time to build a new fence.

Did you hear the story about the peacock?

It's a beautiful tail!

What do you get if you cross a tiger with a kangaroo?

A stripy jumper.

Patient: "Doctor, Doctor, I keep losing my memory."

Doctor: "When did you first notice this?"

Patient: "When did I first notice what?"

What did one flea say to the other flea?

"Shall we walk or shall we take the dog?"

"Waiter, this food tastes funny."

"Then why aren't you laughing, sir?"

What would you bring on holiday if you had two left feet?

Flip flips

Why is a tomato round and red?

Because if it was long and green it would be a cucumber.

"Waiter, will my pizza be long?"

"No, sir, it will be round."

How do you make a milkshake?

Give it a good scare.

Teacher: "Where is the English Channel?"

Pupil: "I don't know. I don't get it on my TV."

Dad: "Tom, why aren't you doing well in history"?

Tom:"Because the teacher keeps asking about things that happened before I was born!"

Teacher: "Tom, I told you to go to the end of the line."

Tom: "I did, Miss, but there was already someone there."

What did one eye say to the other?

"Between you and me, something smells."

I was building a bridge across a river when I saw someone doing it on the other side.

It was my arch rival.

Why did the pony cough?

Because he was a little hoarse.

Why did the toilet paper roll down the hill?

To get to the bottom.

What did the dog say when he sat on sandpaper?

"Ruff!"

What do you call an illegally parked frog?

Toad.

Why are elephants so wrinkled?

Because they are too hard to iron.

What has four wheels, no wings and flies?

A garbage truck.

What did Cinderella say when her photos were not ready?

"Someday my prints will come."

What do pigs put on their sore toes?

Oinkment.

What did zero say to 8?

Nice belt.

What is red and invisible?

No tomatoes.

Why couldn't the chicken find her eggs?

Because she mislaid them.

What do you call a woman who throws her bills in the fire?

Bernadette.

What lies on its back, 100 feet in the air?

A dead centipede

What do you call your mum's angry French sister?

Croissaunt

Why did the student eat his homework?

Because the teacher told him it was a piece of cake!

What do you call a boy...

...with a spade in his back?

Doug.

...when you take the spade out?

Douglas.

...who cannot stand?

Neil.

...with no lower leg?

Tony.

...with a seagull on his head?

Cliff.

...who stands outside your front door all day?

Matt

...in a bush?

Russell.

What do you call a girl with a frog on her head?

Lily.

Knock Knock.

Who's there?

Europe.

Europe who?

No, Europe who! (You're a poo!)

Tom: *"Sophie, you're stupid."*

Tom's Mum: "Say you're sorry, Tom!"

Tom: "I'm sorry you're stupid, Sophie!"

CHAPTER FIVE

WAYS TO BE THE CENTRE OF ATTENTION

We all love to be the centre of attention and have people hanging on our every word (even if we don't admit it). The following games and questions will have everyone interested. They will challenge your friends and family, and some of the questions will have them arguing with each other, while you sit back and enjoy the show!

HOW WELL DO YOU KNOW YOUR PARENTS?

At a family gathering, take out these questions. You may be surprised how much you don't know about your parents.

How did your parents meet?

_____

Where was your dad born?

_____

Where was your mum born?

_____

Where did your parents get married, or did they get married at all?

_____

Do you know how you got your name? What other names were considered for you?

_____

Who in your family do you resemble the most?

_____

Who in the family do you act most like?

_____

Did your dad or mum ever break a bone or have a serious illness?

_____

Did your mum and dad enjoy school? Do you know which schools they went to?

_____

What were the worst jobs your parents had when they were young?

_____

Name any awards your parents received when they were young?

_____

Did your parents have a favourite teacher at school?

_____

What is the boldest thing your parents have ever done?

_____

YOU MAY FIND OUT THAT YOUR MUM OR DAD OR OTHER ADULTS WERE NOT UNLIKE YOU WHEN THEY WERE YOUNG!

MOST LIKELY TO . . .

This is a great game to see what others think of you and your friends, what their strengths are, what they think they might become, who is naughty and who is nice! So ask a friend:

Which of our friends/cousins/classmates is most likely to . . .

Become president?

_____

Be the first to get a tattoo? (which for the record is a bad idea!)

_____

Set a world record?

_____

Represent their country in sport?

_____

Become a millionaire?

_____

Rob a bank?

_____

Streak in public?

_____

Run away with the circus?

_____

Be on the top 10 most wanted list?

_____

Get married?

_____

Be first to appear on television?

_____

Be bitten by a dog?

_____

Write a book?

_____

Do stand-up comedy?

_____

Have plastic surgery?

_____

Attend the Oscars?

_____

Have their phone stolen?

_____

Adopt a child?

_____

Go to outer space?

_____

Give up the internet for a whole month?

_____

Fart in a job interview?

_____

Meet a ghost?

_____

Do a sky-dive?

_____

Have a pet snake?

_____

Fly a helicopter?

_____

Make a prank call?

_____

Get caught in a hurricane?

_____

Own a teddy bear when they are an adult?

_____

Have a crush on their teacher?

_____

Answer their phone during class?

_____

HOW WELL DO YOU KNOW THEM?

This is a great family game to play to learn how much husbands and wives or boyfriends and girlfriends might know about each other. The rules are as follows: you ask one person questions and the other one has to write down their answer. The team with the most correct guesses wins.

» What is their lucky number?

» What is their favourite takeaway food?

» If they see a spider, do they scream, kill it, run away or capture and release?

» If they were in a play, would they be the lead, have a non-speaking part, be the main support or have a small funny part?

» What is their exact height?

» Who texts them the most?

» What is their favourite board game, or do they dislike board games?

» What reason would they give for being late: phone call, work, traffic, they wouldn't be late?

- » What is their shoe size?

- » Would they prefer to be immortal or know they would die at 69?

- » Would they be able to name three countries that start with the letter K?

- » Would they say that they break the speed limit on a regular basis?

- » How many keys are on their key ring?

- » How many boyfriends/ girlfriends have they had?

- » What is their favourite flavour of crisps?

- » If they were on 'Who Wants to be a Millionaire', who would their "phone a friend" be?

TIP

You can add lots of questions and play again. Have a pen and paper to hand, so when the answer is given the guessing partner can turn it over to see if they were right.

HOW WELL DO YOU KNOW YOUR BEST FRIEND?

Use these questions to see if you qualify as best mates or distant strangers. No pressure but it is scored below. So get two friends in a room and test them with these questions.

- » What city were they born in?
- » What is their favourite colour?
- » Are they superstitious?
- » Have they ever been sent to the principal's office?
- » What do they have for breakfast most mornings?
- » Do they get carsick?
- » Do they like scary movies?
- » Are they double-jointed anywhere?
- » Have they ever broken a bone?
- » Do they like peanut butter?
- » What is their favourite junk food?
- » Would they prefer to live without television or chocolate for a month?
- » What is their favourite song of all time?

» If they could have one of the following superpowers which would they pick: invisibility, the ability to fly or the ability to stop time?

» How would they describe themselves in one word?

» What do they grumble most about: school, phones, food or family?

» How many times a week do they wash their hair?

» Which of these smells are their favourite: mowed grass, lavender, the seaside, bread straight out of the oven, a petrol station?

» What would annoy them most: if you were vain, scruffy, over-confident or a dunce?

Count up the answers and give yourself a point for every correct answer:

0-1: Have you guys met before?

2-5: I am sorry to say you need better friends.

5-8: Not bad, but a lot to work on.

8-12: Good friends, but still a few things you need to know about each other.

13-19: You are best friends. Phew!

HAVE YOU EVER . . . ?

"Have you ever" is great to do around a table with one person asking the questions and others guessing what the person will say before they give their answer. You can find out a lot about people and they will find out a lot about you too. This can be great game to play with adults. If they promise to be honest, you never know what you might find out!

Have you ever . . .

» eaten anything that has been on the ground for more than 30 seconds?

» taken anything from the bin and eaten it?

» used the shower nozzle as a microphone and sung in the shower?

» gone for a pee outdoors?

» broken something and blamed someone else?

» farted in a lift with others present?

» burped during class?

» been kissed on the lips by a relative older than 75?

» changed a nappy?

» pinched a person younger than you?

» bitten someone when you were older than five years old?

» peed in a swimming pool?

» done something illegal? (Remember, lots of things are illegal, such as spitting on the street or littering).

» drank out-of-date milk?

» stayed awake for twenty-four hours?

» met a celebrity?

» slept on a waterbed?

» got sick on someone else when you were older than five years old?

» walked into a glass door?

» walked in on a stranger when they were sitting on the toilet?

» laughed so hard you let out a little pee?

» given someone else a bad haircut?

» worn the same pair of underwear for more than a week?

Note: This is a game you can only lose by admitting too much!

THE MATES' QUIZ

This is a quiz you can give your friends and it will give you an idea of the way they think. You may be surprised about some of their answers.

If you were a teacher and could teach your students any topic, what would you teach them?

_____

What is your favourite memory and why?

_____

Who is the one person you trust the most?

_____

If you could have picked your own name, what would it be?

_____

If you could change one thing about school, what would it be?

_____

What is the most enjoyable thing we have done together in the last three years?

_____

Describe a day you would like to live over and over again.

_____

If you did not need to work, what would you want to do as an adult?

_____

What is your favourite thing in the world to do? Why?

_____

Describe your most embarrassing moment.

_____

Do you think you should be nice to people even if they are not nice to you?

_____

If you could have a character from a book as a best friend, who would it be?

_____

Where do you think you will live when you grow up?

_____

If someone gave you a present you did not want or like, how would you respond?

_____

Do you have a fear you would like to overcome?

_____

What new skill do you wish you could learn?

_____

Is it more likely that ghosts or aliens are real?

_____

You can invite three famous people (alive or dead) to dinner. Who would you invite and why?

_____

What personality traits do your parents have that you hope to have when you are older?

_____

If you could invent any machine, what would that machine do?

_____

What was your favourite thing that you learned this year, either in school or outside of it?

_____

What personality trait has gotten you into the most trouble?

_____

Is there something you wish you had said sorry for but never did?

_____

Are your two feet the same or different sizes?

_____

MORAL DILEMMA

Ask someone older than you the following problem. There are two parts to it, but do not tell this to them.

A train is racing towards five people who are tied to a train track. If the train is not stopped, it will definitely kill all five of them. You are passing by and you have the ability to flick a switch that will divert the train to a different track. However, there is one person tied to that track, so if you flick the switch, this one person will certainly die. Do you flick the switch or let it stay on the track and kill the five people?

Discuss the problem with your friend. Some people immediately say they would flick the switch so that one person would die instead of five. Others say that if they did nothing, five people would die but it was not their fault. However, if they flicked the switch, they would be killing one person. So it is not an easy answer. After they have decided, ask them part two.

This time the train is again heading towards five people who are tied to the track. You are on a bridge looking down at the track, and a tall stranger is standing next to you. If you push him off the bridge, he will fall onto the track and, although he will die, he will definitely stop the train, saving five lives. Would you push him?

Discuss the problem again. If they ask whether they know any of the people, the answer is no.

Note: This is a philosophical question and there is no right answer, but more people say they would flick the switch than say they would push the stranger, even though they would be killing one person in both scenarios.

THE PSYCHOPATH TEST

This one question was used in the 1970s to see if someone thought like a psychopath. See if you can answer the question. If you get it right, it may not be good news for you! Try it on others too. You will be surprised how eager people are to know if they are a psychopath or not.

Two sisters go to their mother's funeral. At the funeral, one of the sisters meets a man she does not know. She thinks this man is the perfect match for her and she falls in love with him immediately. However, she never asks for his name or number, and afterwards she cannot find anyone who knows who he is. A few days later, the girl kills her own sister.

Question: Why did she kill her sister? Before you look at the answer, think about it for a while.

Answer:

She reckoned that if the man attended her mother's funeral, he would likely come to another family funeral, so she killed her sister. This is one question you will be happy you got wrong! Apparently if you did answer this correctly, you think like a psychopath!

118

BATHTUB TEST

This test reveals if you are gifted. When you hear this problem, you must answer correctly within two seconds to be considered gifted.

Question: A bathtub is filled with water and you are offered a teaspoon, a teacup or a bucket. You must empty the bathtub quickly. What would you do?

Answer: Most people think it is obvious and say, "I would choose the bucket."

Look at them and say, "A normal person would pull the plug. I am sorry. You are not gifted!"

THE MONTY HALL PROBLEM

This is a famous fun maths problem, but be careful asking this one as it drives people crazy and they will tell you repeatedly that you are wrong. So be prepared for people not believing you until they search the internet and realise you were right!

Imagine you're on a game show and you're given the choice of three doors. Behind one door is a car. Behind the other two doors are goats. You are asked to pick a door and you obviously want to choose the one with the car behind it.

You pick a door, say number 1, and the host of the show, who knows what's behind each door, opens another door, say number 3, which has a goat behind it. He then says to you, "Now that you know it is not door number 3, would you like to stick to your answer of door number 1 or would you like to switch to door number 2?"

Question: Should you switch your choice?

Answer: Nearly everyone will think it makes no difference if you switch or not, and most people like to stick to their original choice. But the answer is you should always switch to the other door.

This is why you should switch: in the first part there was a one in three chance of being right. That means the other two doors together represent a two in three chance of being right. The host has opened one of the two doors and it is not the right one. Therefore the other door now represents a two in three chance of being right. Confused? Don't worry nearly everyone is, but it is right!

THE BANANA TEST

There is a very, very tall coconut tree. Four animals - a lion, a chimpanzee, a giraffe, and an eagle - pass by the tree. They decide to compete to see who is the fastest to get a banana off the tree. Who do you think will win? Your answer will give a good insight into your personality, so think carefully and try and answer within 30 seconds.

If you picked the lion, you are an idiot.

If you picked the eagle, you are silly.

If you picked the giraffe, you have lost your mind.

If you picked the chimpanzee, you are just as stupid as the others.

Answer:

A coconut tree does not have bananas!

THE PRISONER DILEMMA

Two criminals - John and Mary - are caught, arrested and put in prison. They are held in solitary confinement, with no way of speaking to or exchanging messages with the other. The prosecutor does not have enough evidence to convict John and Mary, so they offer each of them a bargain. John and Mary can either betray the other by saying that he or she committed the crime, or they can cooperate with the other by remaining silent. Here is the offer:

» If John and Mary each betray the other, both of them will serve five years in prison.

» If John betrays Mary but Mary remains silent (or vice versa), John will be set free and Mary will serve ten years in prison

» If John and Mary both remain silent, both of them will serve just six months in prison.

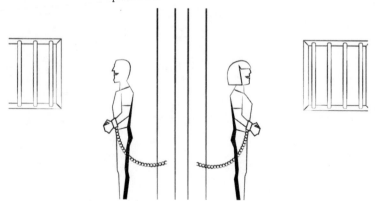

Answer. There is no right answer but it is funny to see how many people are happy to betray their partner in crime!

THE MONEY AUCTION

Ivor Lott comes up with a plan to make money. He plans to auction off euro coins at an auction. While it sounds like a silly plan, there are some rules. The euro coins will be won by the highest bidder, but whoever bids the next highest bid also has to pay what they bid. However, the second-highest bidder gets nothing in return.

So if one person bids 20 cent and the second person bids 21 cent then the second person wins the euro coin for 21 cent. But the first person has to pay 20 cent for nothing.

Have a go and see what unfolds. Ask people to start small and not bid up too high just for the first one. What you will see is that very quickly whoever is the second-highest bidder will outbid the highest bidder, knowing if they don't they will have to hand over cash and get nothing in return.

The most bizarre thing that happens is if someone bids €1 and therefore makes no money, it still makes sense for the second-highest bidder - let's say they bid 90 cent - to bid again so they don't have to hand over 90 cent. So how high could it go?

DO YOU TAKE THE 10 MILLION?

Someone tells you that you need to make a decision in 10 seconds. They take a chessboard out and say they are putting one cent on the first square and doubling it for the second square and doubling it again for each square afterwards. So it will be four cents on the third square, eight cents on the fourth square, and so on. Would you take the €10 million or would you take the amount on the thirty-second square?

If you chose the €10 million instead of the amount on the thirty-second square, would you take the amount on the sixty-fourth square?

Answer. You will be amazed to know that by square 32, the amount is more than €20 million and by square 64 the number is huge – 184,467,440,737,095,516. If you put this amount of cents in a pile, it would be higher than Mount Everest!

FUNFAIR PROBLEM

A boy is taken to a funfair by his mum. It is his tenth birthday and his mum has promised him that he can go on any four rides. As they approach the gate, his mum discovers that she's forgotten her wallet. This is the last day of the funfair and it is too far for them to go home again and come back before it closes. His mum counts the change in her pockets and tells her son that she has enough money to pay the entrance fee and they can go inside and look at all the rides and the parade, but she doesn't have enough money for rides.

Alternatively, the boy could lie about his age and say he was nine and get in for half price, which would leave enough money for the four rides. They walk to the gate and the ticket seller asks the boy, "How old are you?" What should he say?

What would you do in this situation?

126

OBEDIENCE AND AUTHORITY

You are in an art class at school and the teacher tells the class that today each child is to paint a painting of their best friend in the class. The class feels uncomfortable with this, and one student points out to the teacher that some kids will have lots of kids painting them, and other kids won't be chosen at all. The teacher insists that the students should do what she has told them to. Almost all of the students don't want to do this.

Is it disrespectful to disagree with your teacher and can you disagree and still be respectful?

RANDOM QUESTIONS

» A relative is dying and they feel money is the reason there was so much misery in the world. They ask you to take their money and burn it. You promise you will. Would you do it after your relative dies? If you don't do it, does it count as breaking a promise?

» You are spending the afternoon with a friend of yours who isn't very popular. You run into a group of your friends who invite you to go to a movie, but they say that your unpopular friend can't come. What is the right thing to do?

» If all the molecules that make up your body today are different from the ones that made up your body seven years ago, are you still the same person today?

» If a boat is gradually replaced, plank by plank, screw by screw until every single part of the boat has eventually been replaced by a new part over 40 years, is it the same boat or a different boat?

» If a job ad says "must be fluent in French" why don't they post the entire ad in French, that way only genuinely fluent people could apply?

» You find the diary of a friend and it falls open. Is it ever OK to read a page of it? What if you are worried about your friend and you think reading about their thoughts may help?

» If you are all powerful, can you make a rock that you cannot lift?

» If you punch yourself and it does not hurt, does this mean that you are very strong or very weak?

» Are history classes going to get longer and harder the further into the future we go?

» How do vampires always look so neat and tidy even though they cannot see themselves in the mirror?

DESERT TEST

Imagine that you are in a desert and you have with you the following five animals: a lion, a cow, a horse, a sheep and a monkey. To escape the desert, you must abandon one of the animals.

Which one do you abandon?

You have four animals left. The desert is burning up! It goes on for miles. Sand is everywhere. You realise that to get out of the desert, you are going to have abandon another animal.

Which do you abandon?

You have three animals left. All your water is gone so you have no choice but to abandon another animal.

Which do you abandon?

You have two animals left. OK, it's a long, hot walk. You can see the edge of the desert way on the horizon. Unfortunately, you can only leave the desert with ONE animal. Which one do you abandon and which one do you keep?

Before looking at the answers, make sure you know in what order you abandoned the animals.

Based on Japanese legend, the desert represents a hardship. Each of the animals represent an aspect of your life. The order in which you abandon the animals is said to represent the importance of these things to you. The one that you sacrificed first is the least important, and the one that you kept is the most important.

» The monkey represents your children.

» The sheep represents friendship.

» The cow represents basic needs.

» The lion represents pride.

» The horse represents your passion.

Note: This test is for entertainment only. It is not scientific!

CHAPTER SIX

CODEBREAKING, FORTUNE TELLING AND FUN WITH WORDS

Words can be great fun. You can disguise them, work out someone's personality or find out your true love. There are words that you never knew existed and words that are impossible to say together. Read on!

SIMPLE CODE

Codes are a great way to send messages to others without anyone who accidentally sees them being able to figure out what you have said. Here is a very simple code to start with. Once you and your friend both know it, start passing notes and let someone "accidentally" see you. See what they say when they pick up a message that makes no sense to them!

Write out the alphabet across a page and underneath each letter write down the alphabet again but this time backwards so the letter Z is under the letter A and the letter Y is under B and so on. Now write down a sentence and using the code chart change the letters. Here is an example:

A	B	C	D	E	F	G	H	I	J	K	L	M	N	O	P	Q	R	S	T	U	V	W	X	Y	Z
Z	Y	X	W	V	U	T	S	R	Q	P	O	N	M	L	K	J	I	H	G	F	E	D	C	B	A

Code: BLF ZIV Z XLWVYIVZPVI

Answer: YOU ARE A CODEBREAKER

134

PIGPEN CODE

This is a more complicated code because you will always need to stay one step ahead of others. The pigpen code changes letters to symbols using the grid below. Once you have the grid you can write anything that you and your friend can understand but no one else will. It's great for passing notes at school!

Below is the code, each letter is represented by a symbol.

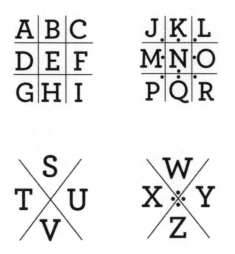

Here's an example:

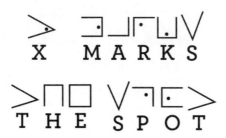

INTERESTING WORDS

It is always nice to be able to casually come out with words others do not know. Here is a list of words you should try to casually throw into conversation.

Ferule: the metal band that holds the rubber to the pencil. It is also a ruler-shaped instrument, generally used to slap naughty children in days gone by!

Mucophagy: the medical term for snot eating. You can inform your friend next time he has his finger up his nose!

Zarf: a holder for a hot cup of coffee or tea (it also sounds like a character from a Dr Seuss book).

Tragus: the little lump of flesh in front of the ear. See if you can find yours.

Ophryon: the space between your eyebrows. They say if there is no space between them there is a chance the person is a werewolf!

Obdormition: when an arm or a leg goes to sleep as a result of sitting or lying on it.

Borborygmus: a rumbling in the lower intestines. Next time you hear someone's stomach grumble ask them to stop with the borborygmus! A stomach rumble is also called a stomach wamble!

Hornswoggle: to swindle or cheat someone.

Misophonia: the irritation you feel with someone who is eating or breathing too loudly.

Groaking: to watch people eating in the hope that they will offer you some.

FINDING YOUR TRUE LOVE

I am not saying this will work every time, but your friends will certainly always be interested in any technique that can help them identify their true love!

Here's what to do:

» Take an apple that has the stem still attached.

» Twist the stem of the apple and recite the alphabet until the stem breaks off.

» The letter you are on when the stem breaks off is the first letter of your true love's name.

» Using the tough end of the stem, twist it against the apple skin until the stem breaks in two reciting the alphabet again as you do this.

» The letter you are on when the stem breaks is the first letter of your true love's surname.

FINDING YOUR TRUE LOVE 2

Here is a fun way to see if two people are meant for each other! Write down two people's names and between the names write the word LOVES

Example: John Smith LOVES Violet Johnson

Now work out how many of the five letters in the word "LOVES" there are in the combined letters of the two names. So, first count how many letter L's there are in both names combined and write down that number, even if it is zero, and do this for all five letters of the word "LOVES" to give you five numbers in a line.

In the example above, there is 1 L, 4 O's, 1 V, 1 E, 2 S's, giving you 14112. Now add the two numbers beside each other to create a new number and repeat until you get to a two-digit number. This is your love percentage!

The two-digit number is the percentage chance that the two people will fall in love. Clearly this is foolproof!

Example:

14112 (1+4=5. 4+1=5. 1+1=2. 1+2=3.)

5523

1075

1712

883

1611

777

1414

555

1010

111

22%

Poor John and Violet only have a 22% chance of love! Sometimes the number never ends and it loops - so the number 998 will never get down to two digits. You can decide if this means infinite love or a complete mismatch whichever is funnier in the circumstance!

MASH GAME

MASH is a two-player paper-and-pencil game, which can predict your future. At the top of the page, start by writing the initials M.A.S.H., an acronym meaning mansion, apartment, shack or house. Write down any categories you want but most people go for things like:

> How much money will I have? Who will I marry?
>
> What type of car will I drive? What job will I do?

Under each of these categories you pick four answers and it is most fun if you pick widely varied answers, so for interest you may say you will get paid:

> 1 cent, €500, €500,000 or €1 billion

Then, one person starts drawing a spiral on a piece of paper and the person whose fortune is being told tells her when to stop. Then you count across the spiral top to bottom to get the magic number for the game. The number is equal to the number of circular lines you have drawn.

You have the number 8 (see the eight dots when you draw a line from one side to another). Now all you do is put your pen on the first answer. So in the example above you would start with 1 cent and you count to 8, moving to the next answer, so 2 would be €500, 3 would be €500,000, and so on. When you get to eight, you stop, and whatever your pencil is on is what gets scratched off. You repeat this until you are left with one answer.

Then repeat the process for the other categories and you have your future - where you will live, what job you will have, how much you will get paid, what you will drive, etc. So you may end up living on the side of the street, earning 1 cent, married to Miss Piggy and driving a tricycle, but hopefully your fortune will be better than that!

INTERESTING FACTS TO SHARE WITH YOUR FRIENDS

» Polo mints can release light when you snap them in the dark.

» Some ribbon worms will eat part of themselves if they cannot find any food.

» It is impossible to lick your own elbow (although it's great to watch people try!).

» Rubbing the groove between your lips and your nose in a circular motion is said to get rid of chocolate cravings.

» Cut an onion in half and rub some of it onto the sole of your foot. In an hour you will taste onion in your mouth.

» The only word in the English language that ends in "mt" is "dreamt".

» There is a city in Norway called Hell.

» Honey is the only food that does not spoil. Honey found by archaeologists in a pharaoh's tomb was found to be still edible. It would have been around 3,000 years old!

» When you say the words 'Forward' or 'Back' your lips move in those directions.

» The first letter of all the continents is the same as the last letter.

» If you are lost in a maze, use the right-hand rule. Place your right hand against the maze wall and keep it there as you walk and you will eventually come out.

» Over two-thirds of the earth's surface is covered by water. If the earth were flat, water would cover everything in a layer two miles deep.

» The Amazon rainforest supplies one-fifth of the world's oxygen.

» Australia is the only continent on earth without an active volcano.

» Thomas Edison, the inventor of the light bulb, was actually afraid of the dark.

» If you slowly pour a teaspoon of salt into a full glass of water, it will not overflow. The water level will actually go down.

» Termites are affected by the vibrations from music. They can eat your house twice as fast if you play them loud music.

» Morton's toe is a condition where your second toe is longer than your big toe.

» Hydroxyzine is a medical drug, but more importantly, it is the only word that includes the letters XYZ in order.

» It is impossible to hum when you close your nose. Try it!

» Look at the corner of your eyes, that little pink part in the corner is called the caruncle.

SAY THESE WORDS

Ask your friends to try and say these words 10 times in a row, fast. It is almost impossible!

» Toy boat

» Yellow leather red leather

» Car park

» Top cop

» Purple paper people

» Good blood, bad blood

» Irish wristwatch

» Flash message flash message

» Red bulb, blue bulb

» Unique New York

THE TEN BEST WORD PHOBIAS

You have more than likely heard of phobias and might even have one yourself. Interestingly, we are born with only two fears - loud noises and falling. All other fears are ones that we learn. The good news, therefore, is we can unlearn them. Here are ten funny ones you may not have heard of:

Coulrophobia: fear of clowns

Gymnophobia: fear of nudity

Paraskavedekatriaphobia: fear of Friday the thirteenth

Panphobia: fear of everything

Pteronophobia: fear of being tickled by feathers

Anatidaephobia: fear that one is being watched by a duck

Arachibutyrophobia: fear of peanut butter sticking to the roof of the mouth

Scolionophobia: fear of school

Phobophobia: fear of phobias

Hippopotomonstrosesquipedaliophobia: fear of long words

And a bonus one: **Aibohpphobia**, spelt the same backwards as forwards is obviously the fear of palindromes!

SAY WHAT YOU SEE

Each number poses a puzzle where the answer is a common saying
or word - you just need to examine the puzzle and say what you see!

1. RADANCINGIN

2. ST4ANCE

3.
```
talk
```

4.
```
LITTLE LITTLE
LATE LATE
```

5. VICE + VICE

6. CI II

7. CHAWHOWHORGE

8. EVELORAT

9.
```
M1YL1I1F1E
```

10. MOUNT MOUNT MOUNT MOUNT MOUNT MOUNT MOUNT
MOUNT MOUNT MOUNT

WORD SEQUENCES

See if your friends can work out what the missing letters are in the following sentences or phrases.

For example: 4 S in the Y = 4 seasons in the year

12 S of the Z

11 P on a F (S) T

12 M in a Y

26 L of the A

7 D of the W

7 W of the W

66 B of the B

52 C in a P (W J)

13 S in the U S F

18 H on a G C

5 T on a F

90 D in a R A

15 P on a R T

3 W on a T

13 is U F S

8 T on an O

29 D in F in a L Y

366 D in a L Y

13 L in a B D

52 W in a Y

9 L of a C

60 M in an H

64 S on a C B

1000 Y in a M

ANSWERS

CHAPTER 1: RIDDLES AND TEASERS

SPORT

1. Second place (if you pass the person in second you are second not first, but nearly everyone will say first!).

2. The fighters are both women.

3. 127. It seems very hard to work out unless you look at it this way - how many losers does there need to be and that is one less than the number of players, so 127 matches. So ,if there are 64 players the answer is 63 matches (because there will be 63 losers).

WORDS

1. Envelope.

2. Neither. The yolk is yellow!

3. Silence.

4. The word "wrong".

TRAVEL

1. The survivors are alive so they are not buried anywhere.

2. It's an electric train - there is no smoke.

3. Your name (we started by asking you to pretend you were a bus driver!).

4. I said every "single" person. He is married.

5. Neither, they would both hit the ocean (remember you're 100 km off the coast of Ireland).

6. All nine - as the tide rises so will the boat.

NUMBERS

1. The other coin is a 5 cent.

2. 21. You only count when two people shake as one handshake. Many will say 42 as they will count the handshake twice.

3. Because all of them are boys. So if all of them are boys then half of them have to be boys!

4. There are three men: a grandfather, a father (the grandfather's son) and the father's son.

5. Once, after that you are subtracting from a number that is not twenty five, its twenty!

6. None - it's a hole.

7. One hour because you take the first one straight away.

8. Nine years - as it doubles every year.

9. 8, 7 from the 49 and then from the 7 he will create one extra. Most people say 7.

FOOD

1. The cup had only coffee granules in it. No water had been added yet.

2. Lunch and dinner.

3. He simply holds the egg more than 2 metres off the floor, so the shell will not break until it has fallen further than 2 metres!

4. Four boys get an apple (one apple for each one of them) and the fifth boy is handed the basket still containing the apple.

5. He was bald.

6. Two apples. What you take is what you have.

ANIMIALS

1. A chess game.

2. None of them. Total darkness means you can't see anything.

3. Polar bears live in the Arctic. Penguins live in the Antarctic.

4. Fourteen. They will think you said 26 sheep, not 20 sick sheep.

5. Never. He will get closer and closer but never get there!

6. Halfway. After he reaches halfway, he is running back out again!

WATER

1. Wet.

2. Nearly drowned. Most people choose nearly saved, which means they are not saved!

3. I said thirty foreheads, not thirty-four heads.

4. Stop imagining.

THE HUMAN BODY

1. Normal. Half of them should be on his right hand.

2. Rib, toe, ear, eye, arm, leg, gum, lip, hip, jaw, bum.

3. Your breath.

TIME

1. They all do. Any month that has 30 or 31 days, clearly also has 28 days.

2. She lives in Australia, where December is in the summer.

3. Each of the 12 months has a second day.

4. The two babies are two of a set of triplets, or quadruplets, or more.

5. What is the time?

6. 12 o'clock. He entered just as the last chime of the 12 chimes rang. Then the clock chimed once for the half hour, once for

one o'clock and once again for the half hour.

MISCELLANEOUS

1. A match.

2. The surgeon was his mother. You will be amazed how many people suggest a priest, or two fathers, and many outlandish answers, without thinking of the obvious.

3. Mount Everest. It just had not been discovered.

4. The name of his horse was Friday.

5. He started out as a billionaire.

6. Glass.

7. 5 cents €1.05 and 5 cents. Most people will automatically say 10 cents!

8. A knight (not night), a baker, a butcher and a bus driver.

CHAPTER 2: TRICKS OF THE MIND

PUZZLE 1: COUNT THE F'S

There are six F's. However, many people see only three. One of the reasons for this is that when you pronounce the word "of" it sounds more like a V sound than an F sound. Try it on others. It only works once on people.

PUZZLE 2: READ THIS SENTENCE

Most people will look at you funny as they will not spot the second "me" in the sentence.

PUZZLE 3: CONNECT THE DOTS

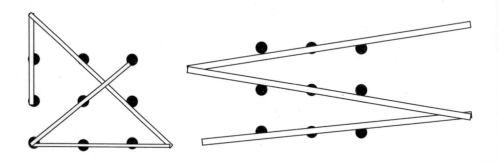

The challenge to this is to literally "think outside the box". As you can see, once you understand that you can go outside the box, it is much easier to achieve.

PUZZLE 4: UNUSUAL SENTENCE

It is the shortest sentence in the English language that contains all 26 letters.

PUZZLE 5: UNUSUAL PARAGRAPH

There is no letter e in the entire paragraph.

PUZZLE 6: A THOUSAND ADDITIONS

The answer is 4,100. You will be amazed how many people say 5,000. Don't believe it? Try it with your calculator.

PUZZLE 7: NINE INTO SIX

They will be looking at how to add an I or a V but the real answer is just to put an "S" in front of the IX.

SIX

PUZZLE 8: ONE LINE AND A NEW NUMBER

It does not seem possible. However if you take the first addition sign, one stroke of the pen changes it from a plus sign (+) to a 4 by adding a line up the side of the cross.

 becomes

PUZZLE 9: MISSING NUMBER

This is a great puzzle. The trick is to look at the numbers upside down. Then you will immediately notice that the missing number is 87.

PUZZLE 10: HARDWARE PROBLEM

He is buying numbers for his house, so each number, from zero to nine, costs the same amount.

PUZZLE 11: THE 9 BALLS PROBLEM

Divide the nine balls into three groups of three. Take any two of the three groups and put them on each side of the scales.

If the scales balance, it means the heavier ball is not on either side of the scale. If one side is heavier, you will know that the heavy ball is one of those three. So you now know that the heavy ball is one of three balls after one weigh. Now take two of the three balls from this group and compare their weights. Using the same logic as before, the heavier ball will either tip the scales or it will be the one you left out.

PUZZLE 12: LIGHT-BULB PROBLEM

You need to think not just of a light bulb being on and off but what else can make a difference. When you think like this you will realise that a light bulb gets very hot when it has been turned on for a while. So turn the first switch on and leave it on for five minutes. Then turn it off. Turn the second one on and leave it on. Leave the last one off. When you enter the room, the light bulb connected to the first switch will still be warm (even though it's off), the bulb connected to the second switch will be on, and the bulb connected to the last switch will be off. This is all the information you need to go into the room only once and figure out which switch belongs to which light bulb.

PUZZLE 13: 4 LITRES

Fill the 3-litre jug to the top and pour the contents into the empty 5-litre jug. Fill the 3-litre jug again, and pour enough into the 5-litre jug so that it is full. That leaves exactly 1 litre left in the 3-litre jug. Now empty the 5-litre jug and pour the remaining 1 litre from the 3-litre jug into the 5-litre jug. Fill the 3-litre jug and pour it into the 5-litre jug.

The 5-litre jug now contains exactly 4 litres.

(There are other solutions to this one too.)

PUZZLE 14: READ THEIR MIND

You may be amazed that eight out of ten people will say carrots. It does not work on everybody, and when I did this on my own daughter, she said "zucchini"!

PUZZLE 15: THINK OF AN OBJECT

The reason this works is that you have flooded their brain with lots of questions so they will generally think of the most obvious colour, which is usually red, and the most obvious tool, which is a hammer. If they think for even a second, it will change the result.

PUZZLE 16: THINK OF A NUMBER

Most people will say 7. Without knowing it, they take 5 away from 12, which makes them think of the number 7. It does not work as well if you ask for a number between 5 and 12.

PUZZLE 17: COLOUR COUNTRY ANIMAL

Most people will come up with this, as they will always have the letter D to start. The number trick always ends up giving you the number four, so if they don't have the number four they did their calculations wrong! Denmark is by far the best-known country beginning with D, but it won't work every time. Most people, when asked for an animal beginning with E, will go for elephant and all elephants are grey. However, you may get a black jackal from Djibouti!

PUZZLE 18: COAST

They nearly always say toast but the correct answer is bread!

PUZZLE 19: SILK

They nearly always say milk but the answer is water!

PUZZLE 20: SMART OR DUMB

Most people will say "What is 2+2?" The correct answer is "Are you smart or dumb?"

CHAPTER 6: CODEBREAKING, FORTUNE TELLING AND FUN WITH WORDS

SAY WHAT YOU SEE

1. Dancing in the rain

2. For instance

3. Small talk

4. Too little too late

5. Advice

6. See eye to eye

7. Who's in charge

8. Elevator out of order

9. For once in my life

10. Mountain (mount-ten)

WORD SEQUENCES

12 signs of the zodiac

11 players on a football (soccer) team

12 months in a year

26 letters of the alphabet

7 days of the week

7 wonders of the world

66 books of the Bible

52 cards in a pack (without jokers)

13 stripes in the United States flag

18 holes on a golf course

5 toes on a foot

90 degrees in a right angle

15 players on a rugby team

3 wheels on a tricycle

13 is unlucky for some

8 tentacles on an octopus

29 days in February in a leap year

366 days in a leap year

13 loaves in a baker's dozen

52 weeks in a year

9 lives of a cat

60 minutes in an hour

64 squares on checkers board

1,000 years in a millennium